ESSENTIAL

INTERNET

SEARCHING
THE INTERNET

MW00685990

ABOUT THIS BOOK

Searching the Internet is an easy-to-follow guide to using your PC to explore the Internet. You will find explanations on everything from understanding the toolbars to choosing a search provider.

THIS BOOK WILL HELP YOU TO GET THE most out of searching the Internet. The book takes you through simple and advanced searching; how to use different search commands; and gives you an overview of the major search engines and directories, as well as telling you the difference between the two. It also gives you details about specialized search providers where you can find people, news, and software.

Within each chapter, you will find subsections that also deal with self-contained procedures. Each of these procedures builds on the knowledge that you will have accumulated by working through the previous chapters.

The chapters and the subsections use a

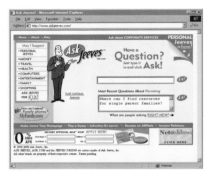

methodical, step-by-step approach. Almost every step is accompanied by an illustration showing how your screen should look.

The book contains several other features that make it easier to absorb the quantity of information that is provided. Cross-references are shown within the text as left- or right-hand page icons: ⌐ and ⌐. The page number within the icon and the reference are shown at the foot of the page.

As well as the step-by-step sections, there are boxes that explain the meaning of unfamiliar terms and abbreviations, and give additional information to take your knowledge beyond that provided on the rest of the page. Finally, at the back, you will find a glossary explaining new terms and a comprehensive index.

For further information, see *Getting Connected*, *Browsing The Web* and *Em@il* in this *Essential Computers* series.

ESSENTIAL DK COMPUTERS

INTERNET

SEARCHING
THE INTERNET

BRIAN COOPER

A Dorling Kindersley Book

Dorling Kindersley
LONDON, NEW YORK, SYDNEY, DELHI,
PARIS, MUNICH, and JOHANNESBURG

Produced for Dorling Kindersley Limited by
Design Revolution, Queens Park Villa,
30 West Drive, Brighton, East Sussex BN2 2GE

EDITORIAL DIRECTOR Ian Whitelaw
SENIOR DESIGNER Andy Ashdown
PROJECT EDITOR John Watson
DESIGNERS Andrew Easton and Paul Bowler

MANAGING ART EDITOR Nigel Duffield
SENIOR EDITOR Mary Lindsay
DTP DESIGNER Jason Little
PRODUCTION CONTROLLER Wendy Penn

Published in the United States by Dorling Kindersley Publishing, Inc.
95 Madison Avenue, New York, New York, 10016

First American Edition, 2000

2 4 6 8 10 9 7 5 3 1

Published in Great Britain by Dorling Kindersley.

A catalog record is available from the Library of Congress.

ISBN 0-7894-6370-9

Color reproduced by First Impressions, London
Printed in Italy by Graphicom

For our complete
catalog visit
www.dk.com

CONTENTS

WINDOW ON THE WEB

The web browser program installed on your PC is the window through which you view the Web. As well as taking you straight to known web addresses, it is the starting point for any search.

SEARCHING EFFICIENTLY

For millions of people around the world, the Internet has become an invaluable treasure house of information, a vast source of software, music, games, pictures, and data. Over the last year or so, it has also become a global online shopping mall. Whatever you're looking for, it's probably available via the Net.

SAVING VALUABLE TIME

Surprisingly, very few people think about how to make their Internet searching as efficient as possible. As a newcomer to the Internet, you may enjoy "surfing" through endless websites in the course of your quest but, as you may already have discovered, a search in its simplest form can return many thousands of suggested websites that would take hours to sift through. As the novelty wears off and the Internet becomes an increasingly essential tool, rather than a new toy, this book will help you to search quickly and efficiently. By following the step-by-step instructions and learning how a variety of search tools work, you will soon be able to:

1 choose the right search tool for the job
2 structure your search queries efficiently
3 become a power user of search tools.

Order out of chaos
The Internet has been described as the new Wild West and, because of its nature, imposing any order is almost impossible. You can, however, impose your own order on this chaos by knowing how to search it.

STARTING FROM THE BROWSER

A web browser is a piece of software installed on your PC that lets you look at (or "browse") different websites. It also enables you to start a search, and will connect you to the search engines that can help you find what you're looking for. The most widely used web browsers are Netscape Navigator and Microsoft Internet Explorer. In the examples shown in this book, we have used Internet Explorer, but they are both excellent browsers. You can have both of them installed on your PC at the same time, and which one you use is a matter of personal preference.

WHAT IS EXPLORER?

Microsoft Internet Explorer comes as a standard part of Windows software and was probably already installed on your computer when it arrived. A suite of Internet-related programs that includes Outlook Express and FrontPage, Internet Explorer enables you to connect to websites and view them, surf the Web using hypertext links, and download programs and files from the Internet to your own computer. By default, its email features operate through Outlook Express, and its Edit feature is directly linked to FrontPage, which can be used to create and publish your own web pages.

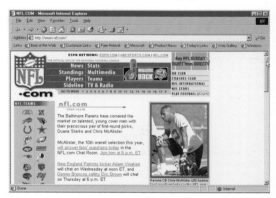

Seen Through Explorer
For more information about all aspects of this program, see Browsing the Web *in the* Essential Computers *series.*

DIFFERENCES IN APPEARANCE

Most websites look the same whatever browser you use. But you might notice small changes if you view the same page using different browsers. This is because the language used for web pages (called Hypertext Markup Language, or HTML) describes how a page appears, and different browsers may interpret the HTML instructions differently.

THE EXPLORER TOOLBARS

It is perfectly possible to use Internet Explorer using only the features provided on the standard buttons toolbar. This toolbar is at the top of the Explorer window and comprises a row of graphically styled buttons. These buttons are shortcuts to features that will help you find your way round the Web quickly, so it is worth spending time familiarizing yourself with the toolbar and learning what each symbol means. Each item on the toolbar is also in the main menus.

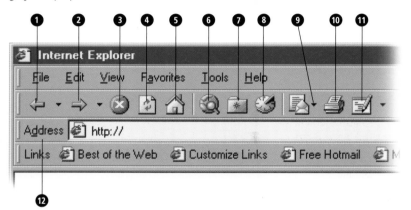

THE STANDARD TOOLBAR

1 Back
2 Forward
These two buttons take you backward and forward through the web pages you have already visited.
3 Stop
Stops a page downloading.
4 Refresh
Refreshes the current page.
5 Home
Loads the default home page.

6 Search
Opens the Search panel in the Explorer window. This gives you access to features that help you connect to search engines.
7 Favorites
Opens the Favorites panel, which allows you to create, access, and manage your favorite sites on the Web.
8 History
Opens the History panel.

9 Mail
Provides a menu of options related to email.
10 Print
Prints the current page.
11 Edit
Allows you to edit the code of the current web page.
12 Address bar
Allows you to type in the address of a known website and go directly to that site.

RUNNING A SIMPLE SEARCH

In the very simplest form of search carried out using Internet Explorer, the search term is typed in, and a designated search engine returns a list of sites. The problem is that there may be thousands of sites with varying degrees of relevance.

1 CHOOSING THE SEARCH BUTTON
● With Internet Explorer running, click the **Search** button on the toolbar. This will create a frame on the left of the browser window.

2 KEYING IN THE SEARCH TERM
● Type a search term in the search text box and click on **Search**. The search begins.
● Note that there is a **Customize** button in this frame. Clicking on this allows you to choose the categories of search and which search engines you wish to use. In this case the search engine is Excite.

3 LIST OF HITS
● When the list of hits appears in the left-hand frame, hold the mouse pointer over any entry to see the address and a brief description of the website. Click any entry to display that site in the main part of the browser window.

4 USING THE ADDRESS BAR

● You can also run a search on the Internet directly from the Internet Explorer address bar by typing **go**, **find,** or **?** followed by the search term.

● After typing your search query, press the [Enter ↵] key. The left-hand "search" panel of the browser window will open, if it is not open already.

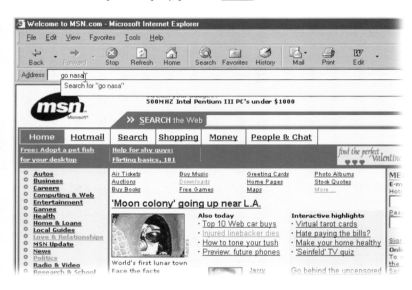

SEARCHING FROM THE DESKTOP

You can access the Internet search tool for your browser at any time by clicking the **Start** button, then choosing **On the Internet** from the drop down **Find** menu. This will launch Internet Explorer if you are not already using it.

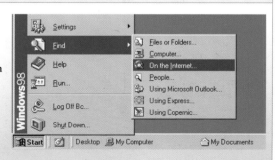

● When searching from the
Address bar, Internet
Explorer will automatically
display the web page that
matches your search term
most closely, as well as
showing a list of hits.
● You may be lucky and
find just the site you want,
but this can be a very hit or
miss method if your search
term is very broad.

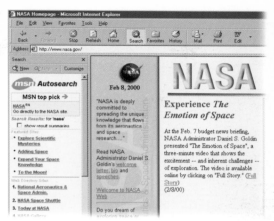

IF THIS METHOD DOESN'T WORK

● You may find that a
search from the Address
bar fails to work in this
way. If so, check that the
options are correctly set.
● From the **Tools** menu
at the top of your screen,
select **Internet Options**
(indicated by a magnifying
glass icon) and then click
on the **Advanced** tab to
bring this page to the front.
Scroll down to **Search from
the Address bar**, and click
on the **Display results, and
go to the most likely site**
radio button if it is not
already selected. Then click
on **OK**.

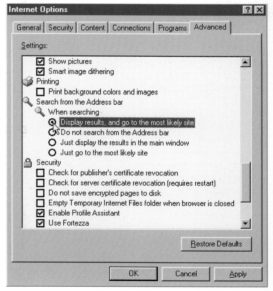

SEARCH TOOLS

Web searching is made possible through the services of search providers, who offer software and databases that are accessed through the web browser or through the provider's website.

WHAT DO SEARCH TOOLS DO?

When you use a search engine, web directory, or Internet search program of any kind, you are never running a "live" search of what is on the Internet at that moment. You are really using a program to interrogate a database owned by the search provider, and which may contain information from millions of pages.

DIFFERENT WAYS OF WORKING

Despite the similarity between the "portal" interfaces of the most visited search tools, you will soon find that search providers return widely differing search results and present them in different ways. This is because the databases on which these engines and directories are based are built and managed in very different ways. The first reason for this is the differing information on the search providers' databases. This information has to be collected, collated, and organized before it is ready for public use, and every search provider carries out these stages in a different way. Some databases are more current than others, or are larger and contain more data. Some search providers can deliver results more quickly than others, and some have more user-friendly or more easily customized interfaces. Some providers are selective in what they collect and may provide site reviews. Others process all the data on a web page regardless of its content or quality, although the database may therefore look as though it is more comprehensive, it may actually be less efficient and offer less useful search results.

Accessing Information
The way in which data is collected, stored, and organized in a database will affect the quality of the results it provides.

DIFFERENT RESULTS

These differences explain why the same search query can produce very different outcomes. Search results from different providers vary in terms of:

- speed of response
- total number of hits
- number of relevant hits
- position of relevant hits
- presentation of hits.

The factors that tend to make us favor one search provider over another relate to the efficiency and usability of the interface. In the end, your choice will usually be determined partly from personal preference for the interface and partly because you want to pick the right tool for a particular type of search. However, there are other important considerations, and these are explained in the following pages.

DIRECTORIES AND ENGINES

One important element that distinguishes one search provider from another is the way they make the information stored in their databases available. Yahoo and Lycos are directory-based , classifying the data like a table of contents, whereas AltaVista and Excite are search engines that rely heavily on their powerful search software.

WEB DIRECTORY OR SEARCH ENGINE?

A web directory is essentially a list of links, usually accompanied by a site description and sometimes a review. The user starts at a top level category, or classification, and then drills down through a series of subcategories until reaching the specific subject area and the required site. A search engine enables a user to search a database created by the search provider.

Speed of search
How long does it take to give useful results?

A search engine provides pages of hits – often thousands of them – arranged by relevance to the query. In either case, the speed with which a particular search tool produces the results you need and the ease with which you can use its tools and access the results are key factors in determining whether or not you use it for your search.

Ease of use
Only using a search tool will show you how easy it is to access its features and the search results.

 14 Web Directories

19 Search Engines

WEB DIRECTORIES

Web page author submits URL to the web directory.

Web site owners submit their site's address, or URL (standing for "Uniform Resource Locator"), to the search engine 🗋. Most search engines and web directories provide a "Submit your Site" option on their main web page to allow the authors of web pages to do this. A reviewer then assesses the page and decides whether to include it in the directory. This process can take several weeks, or even months for some directories.

Web directory reviewer/editor assesses the submission.

Search Provider's Database
If the web reviewer passes the page for inclusion, it will be categorized before being placed in the web directory.

Some web pages are rejected by the reviewer and do not make it into the directory.

Searching the Web
A description and URL for the web page will now appear in the appropriate category.

How Does a Web Page Get There?

HOW DOES A WEB PAGE GET THERE?

Information for web directories is compiled and collated (and often rejected) by reviewers and editors employed by search providers. Most providers offer a step-by-step method for submitting web pages for scrutiny, so this process can best be understood by looking at it from a web page author's point of view. For example, if you had just completed an illustrated history of backgammon, you might want to make it available through the search provider Yahoo! Using the web browser, you would first go to the Yahoo! home page and find the category in which the page should be placed by starting at one of the 14 top-level categories and drilling down to find the most appropriate subcategory for the page.

SUBMITTING THE WEB PAGE

For our backgammon example, this is fairly straightforward as there is a specific Backgammon subcategory within the Recreation>Games>Board Games section of the directory. Having located the appropriate page, all you need to do is click the **Suggest a Site** link at the foot of the screen. It is very important to follow this procedure carefully when registering a site with a search provider like Yahoo! because by giving the site reviewer the most useful information regarding the content and category of your site, you give it the best chance of inclusion in the directory. Directory users are very likely to do precisely what you have just done when looking for sites on backgammon. So your time and effort at this stage will be well-spent to make your site available to users.

- Backgammon Portal - offers concise, targeted backgammon links, rules and tips for beginner to advanced players more.
- British Isles Backgammon Association - offers a calendar of tournaments, results, rules of play, membership info, contacts, and more.
- Can A Fish Taste Twice as Good? - backgammon book; comprehensive study of doubling in an un-even match
- Chicago Point Backgammon Online - an electronic preview of Chicago Point monthly backgammon newsletter, a source of backgammon information for thousands of players worldwide.
- gammon.com
- LadderFacts - provides Yahoo! Backgammon ladder players with info about the ladder, matches & players.
- Nevada Backgammon Association
- Usenet - rec.games.backgammon

Click Here for 101 Useful Websites.

http://add.yahoo.com/fast/add?147960   Internet

The first step in "posting" your site •

MAKING THE LINK

● After clicking **Suggest a link** in Yahoo! you are taken to a step-by-step sequence.

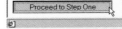

- You have read the brief explanation of how to suggest a site to Yahoo
- You have searched the directory and confirmed that your site is not al
- You have found an appropriate category for your site. (If you haven't explanation for help finding that category.)
- You have clicked on the "Suggest a Site" at the bottom of the page fro

If you answer "Yes" to all of the above, then please:

    Proceed to Step One

● In the online form that appears on screen, type some information about your web page following the bulleted advice below each box.

● This information helps the reviewer to decide whether you have chosen the correct category for your web page.

● The reviewer will then look at your web page and apply the search provider's acceptance criteria before deciding whether or not your page makes it into the directory's database.

Suggest a Site to Yahoo! - Step 1 - Microsoft Internet Explorer

File   Edit   View   Favorites   Tools   Help

Back   Forward   Stop   Refresh   Home   Search   Favorites   History   Mail

Address http://add.yahoo.com/fast/add

Site Information:

Title:

Backgammon through the ages

- Please keep the title brief.
- Use the official business name for the title of a commercial site.
- Please do not use ALL capital letters.
- Please do not including marketing slogans or superlatives (e.g., "The F the Number One Dealer...")

URL:

http://www.myisp.net/users/jsmith/home.htm

- Not sure what this is? It's the address of your site that begins with "htt
- Please supply the entire URL and double check to make sure it is con

Description:

Backgammon was played in ancient Mesopotamia, Greece, and

Always read the Help file...

Always read the Search provider's Help files before submitting a site. As well as helping web authors to promote their sites more efficiently, the Help files will also provide all users with useful information about how the search engine or web directory works. Reading these, in conjunction with the advanced search documentation, will quickly give you an understanding of the directory and make you a power user, which is never a bad thing!

CHANGING A WEB PAGE'S DIRECTORY LISTING

● If you add pages to a website that are likely to change its listing (for example, if your history of backgammon becomes a history of backgammon *and* checkers) you need to inform the directory provider. In the case of Yahoo! you would use the online **change form** option in the **Suggest a Site** page. Web directory reviewers need to be warned when a web page changes so that they can reassess the site and recategorize it.

● As you will see 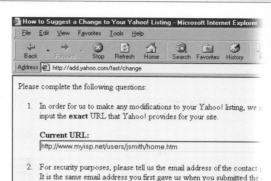, search engines need no input from the web page author because they operate almost completely automatically. If you change your site, most search engines will pick up these changes and amend their databases.

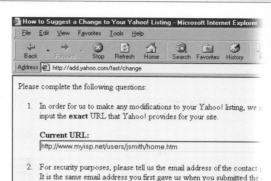

How to Suggest a Change to Your Yahoo! Listing - Microsoft Internet Explorer

File   Edit   View   Favorites   Tools   Help

Back   Forward   Stop   Refresh   Home   Search   Favorites   History

Address http://add.yahoo.com/fast/change

Please complete the following questions:

1. In order for us to make any modifications to your Yahoo! listing, we input the **exact** URL that Yahoo! provides for your site.

   Current URL:
   http://www.myisp.net/users/jsmith/home.htm

2. For security purposes, please tell us the email address of the contact It is the same email address you first gave us when you submitted the

   Current Email:
   jsmith@myisp.net

3. If you want to suggest a change to the title of your site, enter the *new* longer than five (5) words and not all capital letters (e.g. XYZ CORP INTERNET, etc.). For companies, the title MUST be the company something other than its actual name will be ignored.

   New Title:
   History of backgammon and checkers

Done

CONVERGING SERVICES

Yahoo! is, of course, only one of many web directories available free to users on the Web. Many search engine providers now include a web directory on their websites, though on a far more modest scale than the Yahoo! directory. Many directory services now also offer a search engine. Rather than developing these additional services in-house, search providers are now commonly striking up partnership deals with each other, and it is not uncommon for several "rival" web directories to draw on the same database. However, the results are usually processed and presented in different ways, so that it is difficult for most of us to spot the shared connections.

SHARED DIRECTORIES

The directories featured here are evidence that databases are becoming more and more thorough in their coverage of the contents of the Internet, and that these databases are being shared by an ever-growing number of search providers.

THE OPEN DIRECTORY PROJECT

This initiative aims to build a comprehensive directory of the Web using mainly volunteer editors. In fact, at the ODP website (**dmoz.org**), you are encouraged to "Become an Editor." You can choose a topic and, by using the tools provided, add, delete, and update links. The Open Directory Project's data is used by a very large number of search providers including AltaVista, AOL Search, Dogpile, Lycos, Hotbot, and Netscape Search.

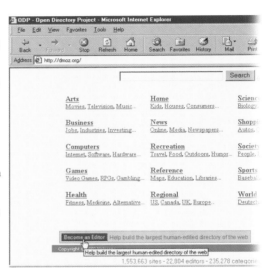

LEADING DIRECTORY PROVIDERS

One powerful directory provider is LookSmart (**www.looksmart.com**), which claims to have a directory of 1.5 million sites indexed into 100,000 categories. It has major players as partners, such as MSN, Netscape NetCenter, Time Warner, and Inktomi.

SEARCH ENGINES

A search engine consists of a database of sites on the Internet, and software (known as spiders, crawlers, worms, or web robots) that endlessly trawl the Internet collecting data to feed back to the database for processing and possible inclusion. Spiders also check out websites submitted to the search engine.

Author's new page is made available on the Internet

The Internet

Author submits the same page to the search engine

The Internet comprises the Web, Usenet, newsgroups, databases, Newsfeeds etc.

Spiders visit web pages that have been submitted by authors and return data to the database

Spiders, unlike their organic counterparts, are searching the Web 24 hours a day locating new data

Search Provider's database
Using the data returned by spiders, the search provider's database accumulates vast records of URLs related to their keywords.

Users search the database by submitting search queries to the search engine

SEARCHING THE LINKS

Search engines collect information for their databases by using software called robots – which are more usually known as spiders or crawlers. Spiders trawl websites collecting information for the search providers' databases.

The information collected will usually vary between search providers. Most spiders find new web pages by following links within documents, and then links within the linked documents, and so on. It obviously doesn't take long to build up a collection of many thousands of URLs based on this simple principle. Different

spiders collect different kinds of data from the web pages (and other information sources) they visit. Spiders are usually programmed to collect all or some of the following elements:

TITLES
The titles of individual web pages as defined by the web-page author.
CONTENT (INITIAL PARAGRAPHS)
The first few paragraphs of any web page.
META TAGS (SEE BELOW)
Hidden content, as defined in META tags.
CONTENT (ENTIRE)
The entire contents of a web page.

META TAGS

META tags are lines of text hidden within a web page's HTML code. The META tags most commonly collected by spiders relate to keywords and description. By default, when a search engine give a description of a website in its list of hits, it shows the opening paragraphs of a web page. However, some search engines will replace this with the description you have specified within the Description META tag.

• *The title tag is the part of an HTML page that is most commonly collected by spiders.*

PROCESSING THE INFORMATION

● Having spidered a website, a search engine processes the information to ensure that searches return relevant hits.

● Some concentrate on the frequency and position of these keywords. Nearly all search engines look for keywords in the pages' titles, heads, subheads, and text in the first paragraphs.

FREQUENCY RATING

● These calculations help give the page a frequency rating for a term. Pages with a high frequency rating are at the top of lists of hits of searches for that term. The rating of pages is usually performed automatically.

RATING BY POPULARITY

● Services like Google base their ratings on a popularity system. A site linked to by many others is judged to be important, and if it is linked to by already important sites, the site is rated even higher.

● As the ranking of sites has no direct human involvement, Google can claim to be both spam- and bias-resistant.

METASEARCH PROGRAMS

Metasearch programs enable you to interrogate a number of search providers simultaneously, and offer both search engines and web directories.

Metasearch providers do not usually own or produce their own databases of websites and URLs. They provide the gateway for simultaneous searches to be carried out on the services with which they deal.

BROAD SEARCHES

● Metasearch programs can be extremely useful if you need to find out how much exists on the Web on a particular topic. For broad searches, they are as useful as anything else on the Web.

● The Metacrawler engine (**www.metacrawler.com**) searches 12 search engines and web directories by default. All you need to do is type your search query in the **What are you looking for?** text box and click on the **Search** button.

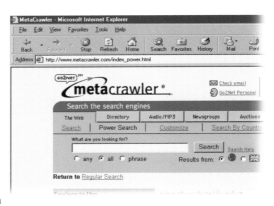

BUILT-IN METASEARCH

● The Microsoft search tool provided with Internet Explorer also has a metasearch option as one of its advanced features.

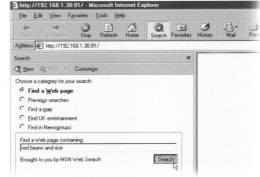

STANDALONE SEARCH PROGRAMS

It is likely that the next year or so will see a big increase in the popularity of *standalone* search agents – in other words, programs that you install on your computer and use as your main (or maybe your only) search tool.

COPERNIC 2000

● The example shown here, Copernic 2000 ◻, functions in many ways as a metasearch engine. Search terms are highlighted in the hits list. Previous searches are saved, if required, in the top frame. This program also enables you to download documents or images for offline browsing.

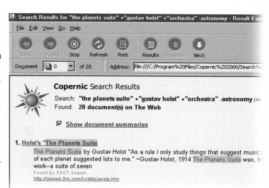

● Updates are carried out automatically including information about engines and categories. Programs like Copernic do not necessarily offer anything that the best web-based search providers cannot offer. But their offline capabilities and the fact that they can connect directly to a wide range of information sources makes them a very interesting alternative for many users.

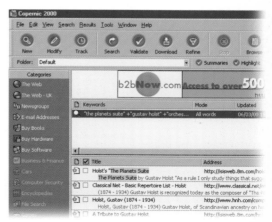

USING SEARCH ENGINES

Ask a bookseller for a book on "entertainment" and you will get, at best, a perplexed frown. Similarly, search engines need a reasonably well-defined query to provide a useful response.

A BASIC SEARCH

Despite some similarities, search engines differ in the way they gather, handle, and deliver information. Nearly all search sites provide advanced search options – usually on separate *advanced search* pages. If you only intend to make a quick search, however, there are ways to modify your query so that you can type it into a standard search box and expect accurate results. In fact, many advanced menus are based on the few simple techniques described over the next few pages.

THE COMMONSENSE APPROACH
The first technique is not really a technique at all – just common sense. If you run a search and get results that are irrelevant, look at what went wrong with your search, then revise your query and resubmit it. You can make use of a first search to gather sufficient information to put together a second search simply by finding out what to include or exclude.

VAGUE SEARCH TERMS
Imagine someone would like to learn more about a piece of music, but all they know is that it comes from the orchestral work *The Planets*. A simple search for **the planets** is not likely to be very successful because the search term is way too broad and vague.

IRRELEVANT HITS

Using AltaVista (www.altavista.com) to search for **the planets** returned nearly 95,000 hits, but without anything relevant in the first pages of hits. The searcher needs to narrow down the search.

RELATED TERMS

Usually a shot-in-the-dark search can be useful in providing a new angle for a second search. The first failed search could suggest using a synonym for the search term, or new words to be added to the initial search term. In this case, nothing obvious occurs. But adding a related term like **orchestra** to the search pays off immediately.

GETTING CLOSER

The search for **the planets** and **orchestra** not only reduces the number of hits by one-third but, more importantly, it brings the most relevant hits to the top of the list. The searcher can now, if required, compile further searches using **Gustav Holst** as part of the search query.

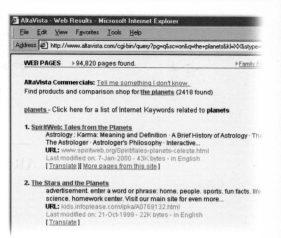

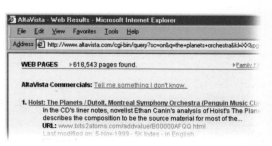

ADVANCED SEARCHING

Basic searches can be adequate for straightforward queries. However, you can greatly increase your chances of finding what you want on the Web by knowing how to carry out more sophisticated searches. By learning some simple "grammar," you can have greater control over the way a search service responds to your requests. The majority of search services let you specify your search criteria in very precise ways, but different services provide these features in different ways.

SEARCH ENGINE MATH

Using math symbols can be the simplest and most effective way to broaden, or narrow, your search. They are accepted at almost every search engine on the Web. The three main search modifiers you can use are:

+ (plus symbol)
- (minus symbol)
"..." (double quotation marks surrounding the search term)

+ SYMBOL
Use the + symbol to introduce additional search terms to your query. Place the + immediately before the additional search term (without leaving a space between them). In this example, **the planets +holst** will search for web pages that contain the words *the planets* and *holst*. This simple device reduces the number of hits from 950,000 to just over 130,000 with the most relevant at the beginning.

- SYMBOL
Use the - symbol to exclude words from your search, for example:
the planets -astronomy.
This searches for sites containing *the planets* but excludes those containing the word *astronomy*.

COMBINING SEARCH MATH

You can use search math queries in any combination. This will probably produce your most effective searches. For example: **gustav holst +the planets suite +orchestra -astronomy** yielded 87 web pages of hits – nearly all of them completely relevant.

EXPERIMENT WITH SEARCH ORDER

As each search engine has its own way of handling queries, it is often worth experimenting with the order in which you submit your query. It doesn't seem logical that this should make much difference, but the search that returned only 87 pages in the previous example returned over 1300 when the order of the search terms were slightly altered.

READ THE README

Search engine math, wildcards, and/or Boolean modifiers may not be universally accepted by search sites, but it is extremely rare for a search engine not to accept either + or AND or - or NOT. At least three search engines will not handle double

quotations, and several more only accept wildcards and other options via their drop-down menu systems. If you don't get the results that these modifiers should provide, either read the advanced instructions for that provider, or simply move to a search engine that accepts them.

Double Quotes

Use the double quote marks around words to be grouped. If your query contains **the planets suite** the search engine will look for web pages containing those words as a phrase.

MORE SEARCH OPTIONS

Many search engines allow you to use an asterisk as a wildcard option in a search. This is useful if your search term has variant spellings. For example, you can type **mandol*** to cater for the two spellings: mandolin and mandoline, as well as including pages devoted to the mandola and mandolinists. It will also return hits for occurrences of the plural form, although most search engines automatically anticipate that you will be interested in plurals for your search terms.

BOOLEAN EXPRESSIONS

You will often encounter the phrase *Boolean modifiers* or *Boolean expressions*. These are essentially a technical way of describing the words AND, OR, NOT, and a few others when used as search modifiers. Boolean expressions are also commonly accepted by search engines, but on the whole you are safer using + (plus) rather than **AND**, and - (minus) rather than the modifier **NOT**. Some, but not all, search engines require you to use upper case when using Boolean logic. To be on the safe side, always use capital letters when entering Boolean expressions.

THE MODIFIERS: AND, NOT, OR, NEAR

AND: All search terms connected by AND will appear (i.e., bread AND cheese).
NOT: To exclude certain words (i.e., bread NOT cheese).
OR: Pages that contain either of two search terms (i.e., bread OR cheese)
NEAR Lets you specify (in numbers of characters) how near one search term is to another on a web page. This term is not widely accepted unless it is submitted as a menu option.
Parentheses allow you to group elements in your search. For example, NOT bread AND cheese means that pages with bread will be rejected but pages containing the word cheese will be returned. NOT (bread AND cheese) will avoid pages that contain both words.

Upper and lower case

By default, search engines look for your search query as upper case or lower case words. If you want to search specifically for upper case words, capitalize them in your search query. But the overwhelming majority of search engines will then look only for upper case occurrences of the search terms you have entered and ignore lower case variants.

DOMAIN NAME SEARCH

With this type of query you can specify that only a certain domain name is searched. For example, if you want to find information about Windows 98 straight from the developers, limit your search to microsoft.com by using the following syntax: **"Windows 98" domain:microsoft.com.**

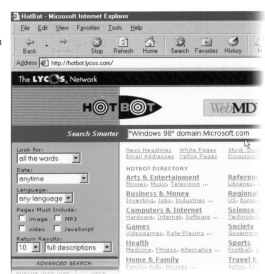

EXCLUSIVE LIST OF HITS

The resulting list of hits is confined exclusively to the numerous websites produced by Microsoft.

1. Internet Explorer Products Download
Main download area for Microsoft Internet Explorer and rela
11/13/1999 http://www.microsoft.com/windows/ie/download/windows.ht
See results from this site only.

2. Microsoft Windows Update
Thank You for your interest in Windows Update Windows U
helps you get the most out of your computer. Windows®
the Windows Update service from the link on your...
9/12/1999 http://windowsupdate.microsoft.com/x86/w98/en/thankssta
See results from this site only.

3. MSDN Online - Windows Logo Program
Adding the Windows Logo to your product indicates to you
tested to meet Microsoft standards for compatibility with
to get the Windows Logo.
3/2/2000 http://msdn.microsoft.com/winlogo
See results from

You can also search for parts of the domain name, for example, to limit your search to sites that have the Australian identifier, type **"your search term" +domain:au.**

USE THE ADVANCED OPTIONS

The following pages show how some of the leading search engines and web directories offer advanced features on their main search pages. These features achieve the same or similar results to using search engine math and Boolean operators, and often much more. The main search page of Hotbot (**www.hotbot.com**) offers all the features described so far. It also has an **Advanced Search** button that allows you to carry out even more detailed searches.

EASIER SEARCHING

It is unlikely that you will need to remember too many of these advanced search terms, other than ones we have looked at so far. Search sites are increasingly making life easier for users by providing useful drop-down menus, help files, check boxes, and other useful tools for users.

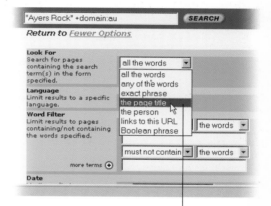

Many advanced features are made available through drop-down menus. In this example, a menu is conveniently placed near the search box and to the right of the directory lists.

TITLE SEARCH

The title of a web page is determined by the words between the TITLE tags in the code of a web page. These words appear in the title bar at the top of the Web browser. To search for web pages by title, use the following syntax: **title:your search term**. This option is unavailable in some search engines.

FORMAT-SPECIFIC SEARCHES

Many search providers supply useful radio buttons and check boxes near the main search box that enable you to specify the format for your search. For example, HotBot (address **hotbot.lycos.com**) has a check box that allows you to specify an images-only search. Here, a search is being carried out for royalty-free images.

*• The **image** check box*

LINKS SEARCH

A links search locates all web pages that contain hyperlinks to the specified web page. This is useful if you are interested in finding out how many people have linked their web pages to your own. The search syntax is: **link:yourwebpage.com**. As with title and domain searches, this advanced search is not accepted by all search engines.

The yellow search box at the top of the AltaVista web page (www.altavista.com) provides tabs that open pages for **Advanced Search** and **Images**, **Audio** and **Video** options. Clicking the **Advanced Search** tab reveals a number of useful options, including a Language box that enables you to specify the language in which the web page hits need to have been written, and two boxes (**From** and **To**) in which you can type a date range for your search.

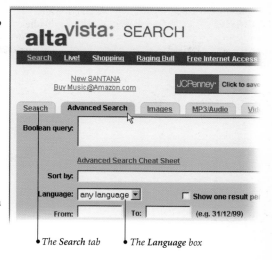

• *The Search tab* • *The Language box*

The **Images, MP3/Audio,** and **Video** tabs at the top of the search box are useful for finding material in a particular format. Click the tab for the format you would like your search term to relate to, then click on the **Search** button.

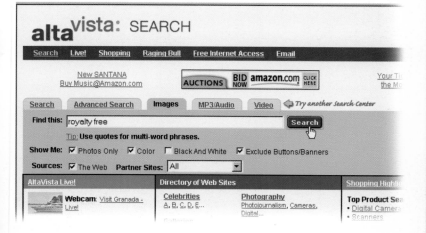

When presenting the results of a search for images, AltaVista doesn't only return a list of hits – it provides thumbnails of all the relevant images too. Click the thumbnail or the links beneath to go to the web page from which the image was retrieved, or to find similar images from other websites.

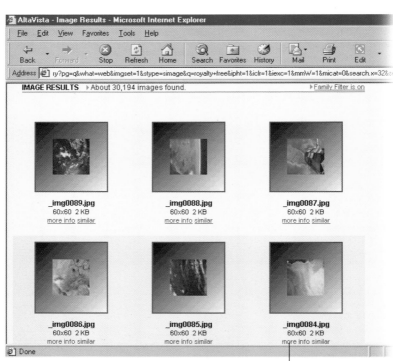

Click the links under any image to go to a web page •

PICTURE FILE FORMATS

The letters .jpg after the images above shows that they are JPEG files. This compressed graphics file format is useful for images containing a lot of color. The GIF format, which you will also come across, is primarily used for displaying images from online sources such as the Internet. It only supports 256 colors, but the files are small and can be used for animating web pages.

FROM ENGINES TO DIRECTORIES

The difference between search engines and web directories is becoming less distinct. It is now usual for search providers to offer a web directory as well as a search box on their main web page. To find information as quickly as possible, the search box and search menus are usually the place to begin. But for those who have a little more time to explore a subject, or who want results that have passed some kind of quality control, a directory can be preferable to a search engine.

This example shows one of the most popular web directories of all – Yahoo! (**www.yahoo.com**) – to look for information once more on Holst. The first stage involves some commonsense choices about the categories in which the composer or piece of music are likely to be found.

Computers & Internet Internet, WWW, Software, Games...	**Reference** Libraries, Dictionaries
Education College and University, K-12...	**Regional** Countries, Regions,
Entertainment Cool Links, Movies, Humor, Music...	**Science** Animals, Astronomy.
Government Elections, Military, Law, Taxes...	**Social Science** Archaeology, Econom
Health	**Society & Cultu**

http://www.yahoo.com/r/mu

After choosing a category, you can begin to refine your search by drilling down to a suitable subcategory. In this example, you might choose **Composition**, and then **Composers**.

- Chats and Forums (212)
- Classifieds (10) NEW!
- Collecting@
- Companies@
- Composition (494) NEW!
- Computer Generated (311)
- Contests, Surveys, Polls (27)
- Cover Art (10)

- Music Therapy@
- Music Videos (31)
- Musicology (35)
- New Releases (5)
- News and Media (
- Organizations (255
- Recording (121)
- Reference (65)

- Composers@
- Computer Generated@
- Interactive Operas@
- Lyrics and Notation (195) NEW!
- Organizations (21) NEW!

- Songwriting (255)
- Theory@
- FAQs (1)
- Usenet (4)

As you drill down further, the appropriate headings become more obvious. Holst is most likely to be found under the heading **Classical**. Eventually, you will find a list of websites that match your search requirements.

Here, the search has reached the end of the directory entries and has reached a website dedicated to classical composers.

The list of classical composers available on this website confirms that you have reached what you are looking for: a large database of composers that contains an entry for **Holst, Gustav.**

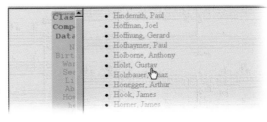

Finally, you have arrived at a biography of Gustav Holst. The principal advantage of using a directory search rather than entering keywords in a search box is that you are presented with many more related options that you can examine during the search. This may lead you to information related to your areas of interest that a straightforward keyword search may not.

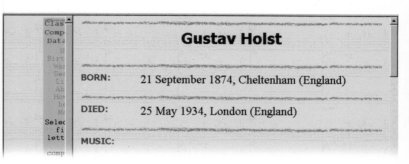

STANDALONE SEARCH PROGRAMS

The latest generation of search software runs directly from your computer rather than via a website. The free search program Copernic 2000 🗋 (available from **www.copernic.com**), is a powerful metasearch tool with some very useful customizable features. For example, it can update automatically its list of search engines while you are browsing. It also enables you to download search results for offline browsing, and will remove duplicates for you.

WHICH SEARCH ENGINE?

This chapter looks at nine of today's most popular search providers describing the main features and showing the web page layout and the results format for each.

WHICH SEARCH TOOL?

You might wonder if there is any need to go looking for another search provider once you have found one that suits your needs. The simple answer is no – as long as you are happy with the accuracy, quality, and currency of the results that the provider returns, and the speed of delivery and the ease of use.

SEVERAL PROVIDERS

Nevertheless, it is advisable to bookmark several web directories and search engines for these reasons:
1 Different search providers almost never return identical results.
2 Search providers can present the results of a search in a variety of very different ways.

Different results
*As the examples show here, the same query ("**gustav holst**" +"**the planets suite**" +**orchestra -astronomy**) submitted to different search engines can return different lists of hits.*
The next chapter explains why these differences in the order and content of the results occur, by looking at how search engines and web directories work.

WHY SEARCHES GO WRONG

The roots of this problem lie in the two methods used to compile databases – by keyword or by concept. Keyword searches collect words in a site that are thought to be important. The problem arises when you enter a word with more than one meaning. If you enter the word "groom," you will be offered sites on horse care and weddings. Concept searches try to work out the meaning of the text rather than just using the specific words. Problems arise when the software working out the meaning of an article containing the word "heart" places it in a medical category when the subject is love.

MetaCrawler Results | Search Query = "gustav holst" +"the planets suite" +orchestra -astronomy - Microsoft Internet Explo

File   Edit   View   Favorites   Tools   Help

Address ⏣ thod=0&cat=Web&target=metaworld&rpp=20&hpe=10&region=0&timeout=0&sort=0&refer=mc-search&format=beta99&swizzled=1 ▾

📖 **Find books on** "gustav holst" +"the planets suite" +orchestra -astronomy **at bn.com**

| View Related: | Web Pages | Directory Listings | Audio/MP3 Files | NewsGroups | Auctions |

Results for ""gustav holst" +"the planets suite" +orchestra -astronomy" 1 to 12 of 12 results

● View by: Relevance | Site | Source   ✉ Email results

Holst, Gustav - The Planets Review
    Classical music fan offers his comments on Holst's suite, the Planets, noting its deep spiritual
    nature and exotic harmonies.
    1000, http://www.looksmart.com/eus1/.../eus315376/eus310254/eus320385 (LookSmart)

$7 trades @ Sc
105+ offices, pe
broker, persona

Classical composer biographies
    This document does not attempt to be a final word on anything. It has always been in a state of
    flux, and I expect it will continue to be so for a while to come.
    1000, http://www.cl.cam.ac.uk/users/mn200/music/composers.html (WebCrawler)

DC's Hotel Sofi
from $89 thru 3/

BH Recording - The Planets (Holst) (1970)
    Bernard Herrmann, London Philharmonic **Orchestra** and Chorus, Chorus master Louis Halsey Recorded at Kingsw
    London, 1970 Released 1970 by Decca/London (more); Liner notes by Harry Halbreich ...
    1000, http://www.uib.no/herrmann/rec/r_pla70x.html (Infoseek)

3AMusic
    Suggested Recording Gustav Holst The Planets /Suite

Search results for : "gustav holst" +"the planets suite" +orchestra -astronomy - Microsoft Internet Explorer

File   Edit   View   Favorites   Tools   Help

Address ⏣ qt=%22gustav+holst%22+%2B%22the+planets+suite%22+%2Borchestra+-astronomy&svx=home_searchbox&sv=IS&lk=noframes ▾

Search results

18 matches Next 10 ≫ | Hide summaries | Sort by date | Ungroup results

1. BH Recording - The Planets (Holst) (1970)
Bernard Herrmann, London Philharmonic **Orchestra** and Chorus, Chorus master Louis Halsey Recorded
at Kingsway Hall, London, 1970 Released 1970 by Decca/London (more); Liner notes by Harry
Halbreich ...
Relevance: 100% Date: 3 Apr 1997, Size 7.4K, http://www.uib.no/herrmann/rec/r_pla70x.html
Find similar pages | 🗀 More results from www.uib.no | Translate this page

SHOP AMAZ
amazon
■ "GUSTAV
■ Buy * Wars
■ Shop 4 Sor

2. Classical Net - Basic Repertoire List - Holst
(1874 - 1934) **Gustav Holst** is recognized today as the composer of "**The Planets**," which remains wildly popular, but for
except perhaps his "St. Paul **Suite**." However, **Holst** was the ...
Relevance: 100% Date: 29 Aug 1999, Size 4.8K, http://www.classical.net/music/comp.lst/holst.html
Find similar pages | 🗀 More results from www.classical.net | Translate this page

3. Colchester Millennium Festival
The new biography of William and Catherine Booth, founders of the Salvation Army, by Lord Roy Hattersley. The first maj
biography of William Booth for 80 years! ...
Relevance: 100% Date: 18 Nov 1999, Size 8.2K, http://www.aspects.net/~alyons/colchester_millennium_festival.htm
Find similar pages | Translate this page

4. Elgar - A Musical Diary for the Next Millennium
If you wish to include any other events in this diary, please e-mail the necessary details to : jnorris@elgar.sonnet.co.uk o
Norris on (UK) 01923 775882 ... Wednesday 12 January 2000.

ALTAVISTA

Opened in 1995, AltaVista is one of the largest web search engines and contains an index of more than 31 million web pages. It has a multilingual search capability using its own *Babel Fish* translation software. This service, which was the first of its kind on the Net, can translate words, phrases, and entire sites.

RESULTS FORMAT

Results include page title, description, date, and options to view more pages from the same site or have the information translated. Other information (e.g., Company factsheet) is offered where appropriate.

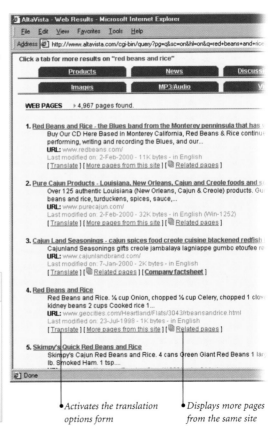

ALTAVISTA FEATURES

- www.altavista.com
- Very large database.
- Online instructions available.
- Relevance to query used to rank results.
- Compact or detailed display of results.

Activates the translation options form

Displays more pages from the same site

Multimedia search features
(images, audio and, video tabs) •

Drop-down menu for
language options •

• Family filter

Advanced •
Search tab

Search box •

Radio •
buttons to
specify search
areas

Directory •
data – mainly
provided by
the Open
Directory
Project

Help files •
and company
information

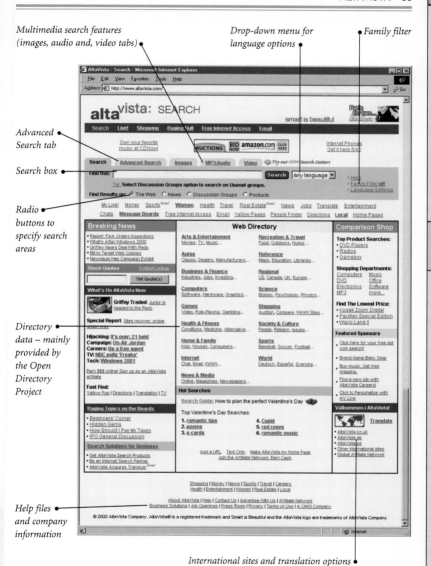

International sites and translation options •

ASK JEEVES

Ask Jeeves is one of several Internet search engines that supports *natural language* queries. Ask Jeeves a question and he will return a list of hits organized into drop-down lists of related sites. Unlike other similar search engines, though, Ask Jeeves provides answers in the form of questions that it hopes will exactly match what you are looking for. According to its owners, every link in the Ask Jeeves knowledge base has been selected by an editor, not by an automated process.

RESULTS FORMAT

Whether your search is a question in plain English or a sequence of words, the answers from Ask Jeeves are in the form of questions. Otherwise, hits for your search term will be organized in further drop-down menus – one for each search engine that has been interrogated.

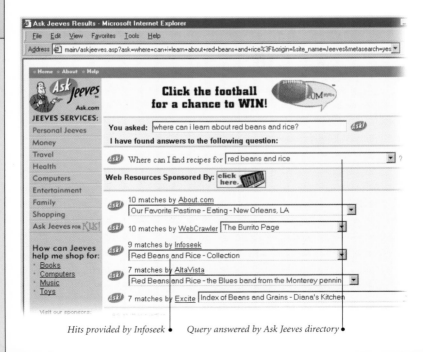

Hits provided by Infoseek •   *Query answered by Ask Jeeves directory* •

ASK JEEVES FEATURES

- www.askjeeves.com
- Queries can be made in natural language.
- Unknown spellings are queried and a spell check is offered.
- Main search provided by Ask Jeeves directory.
- Secondary search (a *metasearch* feature) interrogates leading search engines.
- **Personal Jeeves** feature offers customized information and services.

Type your query as a plain English question (or simply a word, or a string of words) •

Sample search query, recently submitted •

View what other Ask Jeeves users are searching for now •

DOGPILE

Dogpile is among the most popular metasearch engines – an engine that sequentially queries several search engines and web directories. It can access 18 information sources, such as stock prices, yellow pages, and weather forecasts. Information from Usenet newsgroups and other information sources is also available.

CONTROLLING THE SEARCH

Dogpile presents results grouped under individual search providers. Rather than simultaneously interrogating all the search providers, Dogpile submits your query to a selection of providers at a time. Dogpile's advanced search feature enables you to determine the order in which these sources are queried, and to remove information sources from its metasearch list if they are not relevant to your query. By checking the appropriate radio button below the search box, you can specify a search area before hitting the **Fetch** button. After reading the list of hits, you can tell Dogpile to query more search providers by clicking on **Next Set of Search Engines** at the foot of the page.

DOGPILE FEATURES

- **www.dogpile.com**
- Easily customized.
- Large number and variety of information sources queried.
- Useful regional feature for searching locally.
- Specify information source-type before beginning search.
- Also offers directory structure for searching.

Specify the type of information to be retrieved •

Click this tab to set your regional preferences, type • *your City, State and/or Zip Code, and click Save.*

• *Use the Custom Search page to change the order in which the specified search engines are queried.*

• *Link to the Open Directory (Dogpile version)*

GOOGLE

Google's main search page is in stark contrast to the busy portal interface favored by many top search providers.

However, behind the simple, uncluttered interface a very powerful search engine using unique software is at work.

PAGE RANKING

Google's search engine is based on an automated method that ranks web pages according to their relationship with other web pages – with special attention being paid to the links between pages that share

common subjects or themes. Google analyzes the relevance of a page by looking at the pages that link to it. Each link is regarded as a "vote" for that page, and the more votes a page receives, the more highly it is ranked.

SEARCH TERMS AND PROXIMITY

Google only produces results that match all your search terms. It also notes the proximity of the search terms on a page, and prioritizes those hits that place the search terms close to each other.

"I'm feeling lucky"

The developers at Google are very confident of the effectiveness of Google's search capabilities, and they have incorporated a unique feature in their **I'm Feeling Lucky** button.

If you click on this button after entering your search terms, Google will send you straight to the website that emerges at the top of its search results, and many times it is uncannily accurate.

*Google's **I'm feeling lucky** button runs your search and then takes you straight to the web page of the number one hit*

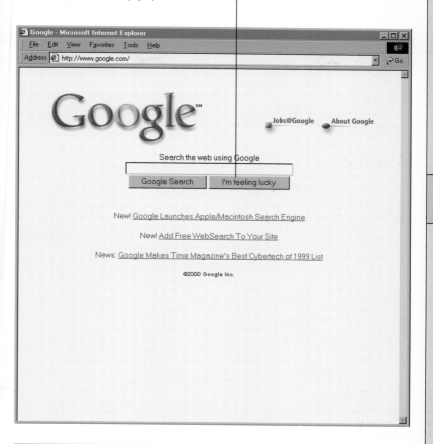

GOOGLE FEATURES

- www.google.com
- Minimalist, uncluttered search screen.

- Unique **I'm Feeling Lucky** button for fast results.

- Has its own software for rating pages.
- Matches all terms used.

HOTBOT

HotBot has been one of the leading search engines since its launch by Wired Digital in 1996. While essentially a search engine, it now provides a directory service using material mainly from the Open Directory. HotBot has proved enormously popular in recent years because of its highly effective user interface. From the main search page, it is easy to fine-tune a search using the drop-down menus in the left-hand panel. With most search engines, you need to access a separate page to set these advanced options. HotBot is also capable of processing plain English queries.

Along with the list of hits, HotBot offers a number of search refinements and other related information likely to be useful to the searcher. In this case, it offers a link to down-loadable music files on the LycosMusic service.

THE LYCOS NETWORK

Since October 1998 HotBot has been part of the Lycos network and is run as a separate service on this network, which offers numerous Net-based services including free email, clubs, chat, a shopping center, and entertainment.

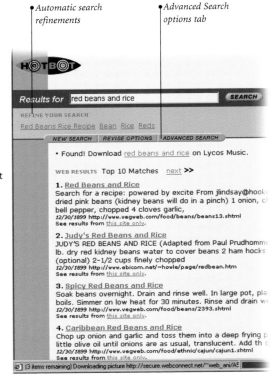

Automatic search refinements

Advanced Search options tab

HOTBOT FEATURES

- **www.hotbot.com**
- Many power-searching options available via drop-down menus from the main interface.
- Indexes more than 110 million web documents.
- Offers natural language construction of searches.

Many advanced search options are available from these drop-down menus(see page 24)

Free email and home pages on offer

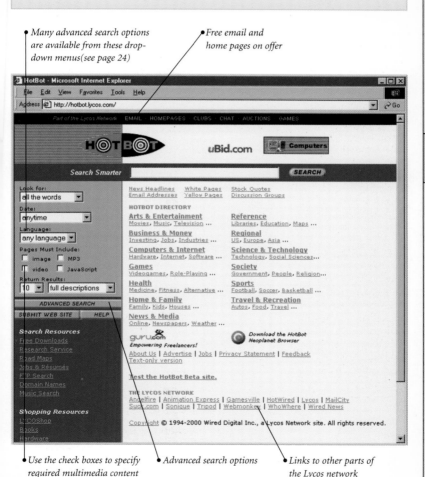

Use the check boxes to specify required multimedia content

Advanced search options

Links to other parts of the Lycos network

LYCOS

Lycos began as a search engine but now boasts a very large directory (with some excellent multimedia areas), which is its primary asset. Its portal interface makes Lycos similar in structure and overall feel to Yahoo! From the main Lycos page you can set up a free email account, organize free Internet access, play online games, chat online, build your own home page, read news headlines and much more. You can also customize the Lycos page to suit your own preferences.

SEARCH RESULTS
These are usefully organized by categories: first by the most popular links, then websites (results mainly drawn from the Open Directory), news articles (from some of the Web's top news sites) and finally shopping (with results from LYCOShop).

IMAGE GALLERY
The excellent searchable image gallery contains more than 80,000 picture files, viewable initially as thumbnails. You can also use Lycos to search the Web specifically for images, audio or video files.

*• The **Popular** heading appears when the Lycos search team have gathered sites appropriate for this search.*

Online help
Lycos provides detailed help files for searching, and for viewing and downloading files in its Image Gallery.

LYCOS FEATURES

- **www.lycos.com**
- Powerful search site with many customizable features.
- **Safe search** parental

control feature.
- Searchable Lycos image gallery and multimedia search feature for the entire Web.

*The **Tools** option lets you specify the areas that you want to be searched*

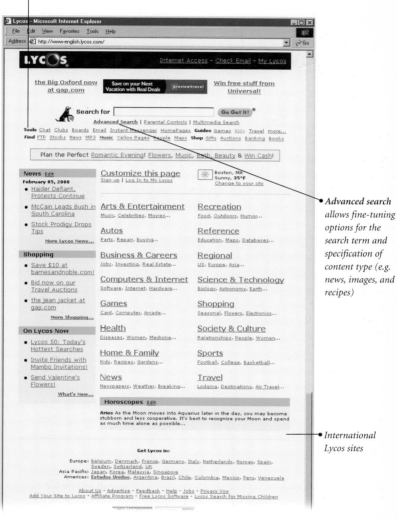

Advanced search allows fine-tuning options for the search term and specification of content type (e.g. news, images, and recipes)

International Lycos sites

27 Search engine math

METACRAWLER

Metacrawler is another major metasearcher from the Lycos network, but unlike Dogpile it presents the results according to relevance, site, or source. MetaCrawler gets its results from a large number of web search engines. It then collates the results and presents them in one long list of hits, arranged according to preferences that are specified in the order of the search terms entered by the user.

WIDEN OR NARROW THE SEARCH

Metacrawler gives the source of the results and provides a brief description of the site of each search provider that has returned a hit. There is also a link to other search providers. A **View Related** feature provides further possible hits as well as an option to narrow the search to various types of search formats.

• *Metacrawler suggests refinements for your search*

• *Email results to a friend option*

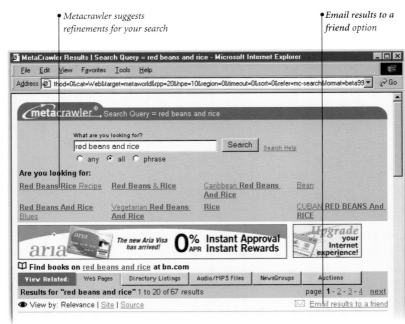

Choose information source-type

Metaspy is a fun feature that lets you take a peek at what other Metacrawler users are searching for at that moment

METACRAWLER FEATURES

- **www.metacrawler.com**
- Create your own customized search page.
- Any duplicate returns are eliminated.
- Offers **Search by country** feature.
- The MiniCrawler feature is a small desktop window of MetaCrawler.
- MetaSpy feature shows other users' queries.

NETSCAPE SEARCH

To access Netscape Search's search page, click **Search Shortcuts** at center-top of the Netscape home page. This all-in-one search page gives easy access to more than 30 different search providers organized according to search type.

SPECIALIST SEARCHES

Netscape's search pages include specialist search providers such as WhoWhere (**www.whowhere.com**) for locating people, and e-commerce-related search tools (such as **wine.com**). Netscape's search service returns four distinct types of data to a search query: Websites, NetCenter pages (relating to content within Netscape NetCenter), website categories (relating to categories within the Open Directory project), and Reviewed websites.

NETSCAPE SEARCH FEATURES

- **www.netscape.com**
- Directory-based engine built by human editors.
- Comprehensive help

files.
- Regularly scanned for dead links.
- Internet Keywords

feature allows quick location of companies' websites simply by entering company name.

Click a search provider to activate it for the current search •

Check this box to make the current search service the default •

Your search term is remembered when you return to this page either to modify the search or to use another service •

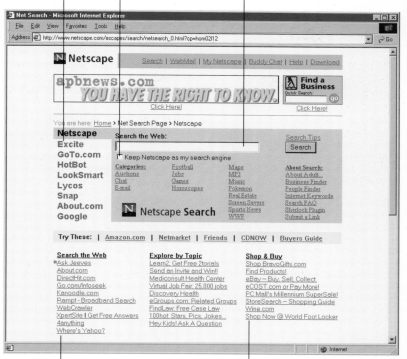

• *Netscape Search offers a wide range of alternative search services*

• *Shop & Buy in Netscape Search provides a comprehensive shopping opportunity*

NORTHERN LIGHT

Northern Light boasts a special collections database comprising over 6000 publications. All information sources are fully searchable so that any successful query will produce a summary of results with appropriate source details.

NORTHERN LIGHT'S CUSTOM SEARCH FOLDERS

Northern Light groups the results of your queries in folders to the left of the browser window. These Custom Search Folders are unique to your search rather than representing the search provider's own web directory categories.

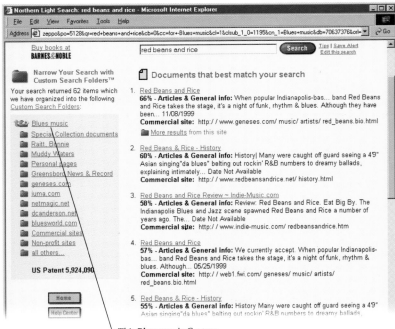

• This **Blues music Custom Search Folder** contains the folders listed beneath it

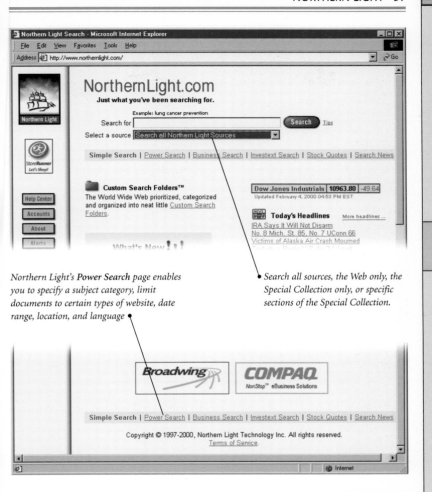

*Northern Light's **Power Search** page enables you to specify a subject category, limit documents to certain types of website, date range, location, and language •*

• Search all sources, the Web only, the Special Collection only, or specific sections of the Special Collection.

NORTHERN LIGHT FEATURES

- **northernlight.com**
- Supports queries made in natural language.

- Special set of over 1600 documents unavailable elsewhere on the Web.

- Custom search folders group returned hits by subject category.

SPECIALIZED SEARCHES

The availability of information and products on the Web has led to the development of countless sites where you can find people, services, news, and software, which we look at here.

ADVANCED OPTIONS

As we have seen in previous chapters, all the most popular search engines provide much more than the basic tools for searching the Web. Nearly all offer advanced options that enable you to search specifically for email addresses, Usenet newsgroup postings, information from news feeds, white and yellow pages, shopping databases, software collections, maps, online shopping, and auctions.

DATABASE INTERROGATION
Since all this information is held on databases owned and maintained by search providers, the source of the material – whether Web, Usenet newsgroup, or commercial telephone listings – is irrelevant. When you run a search from your web browser you are not running a live search of what is on the Internet at that moment, but rather interrogating a database owned by that particular search provider. Some search providers, however, specialize in certain types of information, which we look at in the next few pages.

SEARCHING FOR PEOPLE

Email directories and white pages services are still in their infancy and are not yet fully comprehensive. This means that there is no guarantee you'll find that long-lost neighbor who moved away years ago.

However, if your old neighbor signed up for a free email account and, while doing so, left the box that says **include me in your email directory** checked, he/she may certainly be listed in at least one email directory.

Other providers
Email addresses and white pages data are available as search options from many search providers. You can also run a people search from Microsoft Outlook or Outlook Express.

OUTLOOK EXPRESS

Although Microsoft's email program, Outlook Express, is not primarily a tool for searching the Web, it does include a **Find People** feature. You can use it to find people either locally in your own address book or globally on the Internet.

1 OUTLOOK EXPRESS
● In Outlook Express, click on the **Addresses** button in the toolbar.

2 FIND PEOPLE
● In the **Address Book** window, click on the **Find People** button.

3 SEARCH PROVIDER
● Choose a search provider from the drop-down menu. In this example, the Lycos Network's *WhoWhere? Internet Directory Service* is being used.

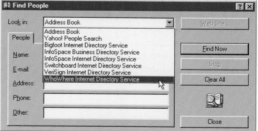

4 FIND NOW
● Type the name of the person you are searching for and click on **Find Now**.

5 BROWSE THE NAMES
● After a short wait, a list of names is compiled for you to browse.

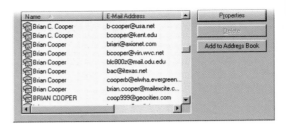

BIGFOOT

Bigfoot (**www.bigfoot.com**) is renowned for its simplicity as a people finder. You can enter just the first and last names of the person you're looking for. However, it also offers a number of options for narrowing down the terms of your search.

1 NAME SEARCH
● Type the name of the person you're looking for, and specify a city if you want to make the search more specific.

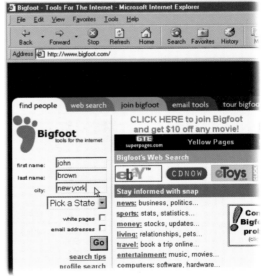

2 PICK STATE

● Click the arrow next to **Pick a State** and choose the relevant state from the menu that appears.

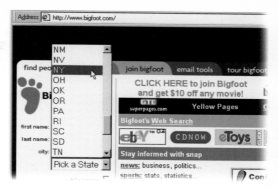

3 CLICK GO

● Check the box next to white pages, email addresses, or both. Then click on **Go**.

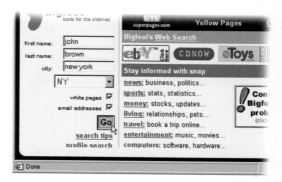

4 DISPLAYING THE RESULTS

● Results appear grouped under email addresses or as white pages entries with the telephone numbers of the people found.

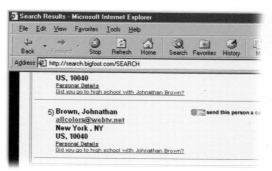

YELLOW PAGES

With the vast explosion in commercial websites – from one-person startups right up to multinationals – and the rise of e-commerce, there has been a corresponding growth on the Web of search sites devoted to finding businesses, their products and services, and the people who make them work.

COMMERCIAL SEARCHES

Once again, many of the main search services provide a perfectly adequate method of searching for such material. All you have to do is choose the yellow pages or white pages (or people or businesses) options and then run your search as usual via the search box.

However, if your favorite search service doesn't give you this option, you could go straight to a search provider who specializes in commercial searches. GTE Superpages.com (**www.superpages.com**) offers an immensely wide range of search options for people, companies, services, products, and much more. In this example, though, we use Ameritech.yellowpages.net (**www.yellowpages.net**) to find out where we could eat an Italian meal during our upcoming trip to Seattle.

1 APPROPRIATE CATEGORY

● Enter **restaurants** in the **Category** box, **Seattle** in the **City** box, select **Washington** from the **State** drop-down menu, and finally click on **Find it!**

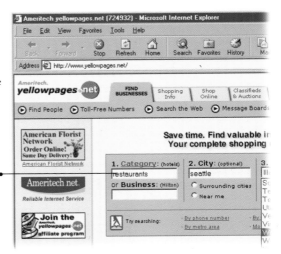

The Category box

2 RELATED CATEGORIES

● Scroll down the list of hits. At the bottom, a list of **Related Categories** appears. Click the appropriate category – in this case, **Restaurants-Italian**.

3 FURTHER INFORMATION

● Click on any restaurant in the list for further information and a map.

A-Z list of Italian restaurants ●

SEARCHING FOR NEWS

To search for postings to Usenet news-groups, use the Usenet option in your favorite search service, if available. This is sometimes accessed via the Advanced search settings, but different search services use different locations.

SIMPLY DOGPILE

In the case of Dogpile, (**www.dogpile.com**), simply click the **Usenet** radio button before clicking on **Fetch** to run your search.

USENET SEARCH

Along with a number of other search services, product details, and a web index, Deja.com offers a vast searchable database of Usenet newsgroup messages including archive material going back several years.

Results are clearly organized making it easy to follow discussion threads within and across the tens of thousands of available newsgroups. Searching for Usenet messages can be as easy as searching the Web.

1 POWER SEARCH

● Deja.com's usenet service is available on **deja.com/usenet**. On this web page, click on **Power Search**. (Unless you have an extremely specific query, using **Quick Search** usually returns too many hits.)

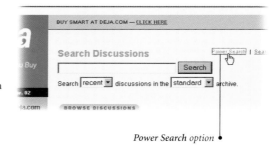

Power Search option ●

2 ENTER KEYWORDS

● On the **Power Search** page, type your query in the **Enter Keywords** box. Explore the options in the drop-down menus under **Limit Search** and choose any that seem appropriate, then click on **Search**.

Type your keyword here ●

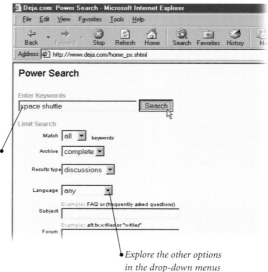

● *Explore the other options in the drop-down menus*

3 READ THE MESSAGE

● When the list of hits appears, click the messages you wish to read. The date of posting, the name of the Usenet newsgroup, and the name of the author also appear in the same line.

List of hits ●

4 CHOOSE OPTIONS

● After reading the message, choose from the list of options below the message, or move to the next or previous message in the list of hits.

CLASSIFICATIONS OF POSTINGS

Usenet postings can fall into one of the following classifications:
alt. Anything goes
rec. Recreational topics

comp. Computer subjects
soc. Social issues
sci. Science subjects
news. Usenet information
biz. Business matters

humanities. The arts
talk. Current debates
regional. Local subjects
k12. Educational issues
misc. The unclassifiable.

SEARCHING FOR SOFTWARE

If you are interested in searching for software or simply browsing for that essential utility, patch, or game, there are many excellent shareware and freeware sites on the Web that will almost certainly have what you are looking for. Most contain a search box and a site directory structure that is as simple to use as any standard search engine.

BROWSE

If you are interested in checking out the latest Internet search software available for Windows, for example, you can simply browse the relevant section of a software download site like **www.winfiles.com**.

1 CHOOSE A CATEGORY

● On the main page of Winfiles.com, click on **Windows Shareware**.

Choose a category ●

2 ENTER KEYWORDS

● The next window contains the category we are looking for, so click on **Windows 95/98 Software**.

3 TOOL SELECTION

● After clicking **Network and Internet Tools** (below), select **Web Browser Tools**.

Network and Internet Tools ●

Web Browser Tools ●

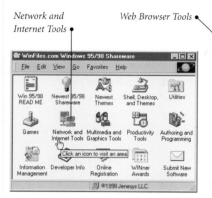

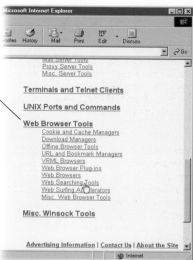

4 SOFTWARE SELECTION

● Scroll down the list of shareware descriptions until you find something that interests you. This example shows the **Copernic2000** program.

Download time ●

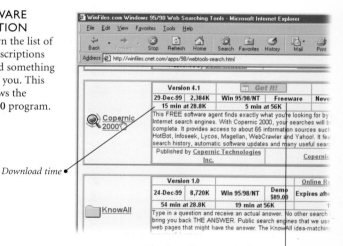

This shows the program's shareware ●
status – in this case it is freeware

USING THE SEARCH BOX

If you know the name of the piece of software you want to download, use the search box provided at the software site.

For example, to find and download the popular email client, Eudora Light, from the Tucows software site, do the following:

1 TYPE THE SEARCH TERM

● Go to Tucows' website (**www.tucows.com**). In the **Search Tucows** window type the search term: **Eudora Light**. If necessary, click the menu in the right-hand box to specify your computer's operating system.

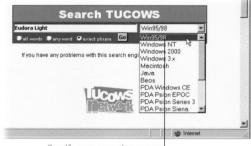

Specify your operating system ●

2 CLICK ON EXACT PHRASE

● Click the **Exact phrase** radio button to search for the complete phrase **Eudora Light**, and click the **Go** button.

3 DOWNLOAD NOW

● Click the **Download Now** button next to the appropriate description. Follow the instructions that appear onscreen regarding download and installation.

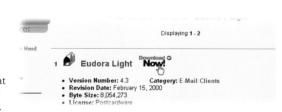

4 CHOOSING A REGIONAL SITE

● Choose a regional site closest to you from which to download.

To ensure faster and more reliable downloads, please choose a site within the continent or region closest to you.
u would like to learn more about the benefits of hosting a TUCOWS affiliate site, click h
Welcome to TUCOWS, the world's best collection of Internet Software.

Please select the country you live in (or the one nearest you).

Pick a Region:

    Africa
    Asia
    Australia
    Canada
    Caribbean
    Central America
    Europe
    South America
    United States

    Continue...

5 CHOOSING A LOCAL SITE

● Specify the site most local to you from which the software is available.

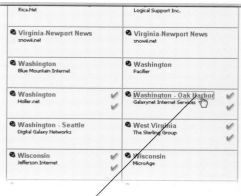

Rica.Net	Logical Support Inc.
Virginia-Newport News snowii.net	**Virginia-Newport News** snowii.net
Washington Blue Mountain Internet	**Washington** Pacifier
Washington Holler.net	**Washington - Oak Harbor** Galaxynet Internet Services
Washington - Seattle Digital Galaxy Networks	**West Virginia** The Sterling Group
Wisconsin Jefferson Internet	**Wisconsin** MicroAge

Selecting the local site ●

6 MONITORING THE DOWNLOAD

● If the download utility **Netzip Download Demon** is installed on your computer, its window opens to monitor the downloading. Once the software is downloaded, it's yours to use.

Netzip Download Demon

PLAYFREEMUSIC   [02] 00:00

peoplesound.com   CLICK HERE →

Click Here

Saving: Eudora43.exe
From: http://galaxynet.tucows.com/files5/Eudora43.exe
To: C:\My Download Files\Eudora43.exe   Powered by...
Status: 1056K of 7865K (7.3 K/sec)
Time left: 15 min, 28 sec   13%

ARTISTdirect.com

    Advanced   Pause   Resume   Cancel

GLOSSARY

BOOLEAN MODIFIERS
Words that help you to modify the terms of a key word search.

BROWSER
See Web browser.

CRAWLER
See Spider

DIAL-UP NETWORKING SOFTWARE
Windows 98 software that enables you to connect to the Internet via a service provider.

DOWNLOAD
The process of file-transfer from a remote computer to your own computer.

EMAIL (ELECTRONIC MAIL)
A system for sending messages between computers that are linked over a network.

HTML (HYPERTEXT MARK-UP LANGUAGE)
The formatting language used to create web pages. HTML specifies how a page should look on screen.

INTERNET SERVICE PROVIDER (ISP)
A commercial organization that provides access to the Internet.

FREEWARE
Software that can be freely used and distributed, but the author retains copyright.

HYPERTEXT
Text that contains links to other parts of a document, or to documents held on another computer. Hypertext links on web pages are usually highlighted or underlined.

HYPERLINKS
A "hot" part of a web page (e.g., text, image, table etc.) that links to another part of the same document or another document on the Internet.

METASEARCH PROGRAM
A program that enables you to query simultaneously the databases of a number of search providers.

MODEM (MODULATOR-DEMODULATOR)
A device that converts between digital and analog signals, and allows computers to send and receive via a telephone line.

NEWSGROUPS
Internet discussion groups on specific topics, where people can post information or contribute to public debates.

NEWSREADER
Software that enables you to access and use newsgroups. Outlook Express has newsreader capabilities.

PLUG-IN
A program that adds features to a web browser so that it can handle files containing, for example, 3D and multimedia elements.

PROTOCOL
A set of rules that two computers must follow when they communicate.

SEARCH DIRECTORY
Database of website URLs and site descriptions organized by category and, in some cases, accompanied by reviews.

SEARCH ENGINE
Software that searches for specific information on the Internet based on your search criteria. The term is commonly applied to websites that host search facilities.

SEARCH PROVIDER
Any organization that provides search services for Internet users.

SERVER
Any computer that allows users to connect to it and share information and resources held on it.

SHAREWARE
Software that is made freely available for use on a try-before-you-buy basis.

SPIDER
A program that search providers use to collect information. Spiders can also be referred to as crawlers, worms, and web robots (or *bots*).

USENET
A network of computer systems that carry the Internet discussion groups called newsgroups.

WEB BROWSER
A program used for viewing and accessing information on the Web.

WORLD WIDE WEB (WWW, W3, THE WEB)
The collection of websites on the Internet.

WORM
See Spider

INDEX

ACKNOWLEDGMENTS

PUBLISHER'S ACKNOWLEDGMENTS
Dorling Kindersley would like to thank the following:
Paul Mattock of APM, Brighton, for commissioned photography.
Microsoft Corporation for permission to reproduce screens
from within Microsoft® Internet Explorer.
altavista.com; askjeeves.com; bigfoot.com; deja.com; directhit.com;
dmoz.org; dogpile.com; excite.com; google.com; hotbot.yahoo.com;
infoseek.com; ooksmart.com; lycos.com (© 2000 Lycos, Inc.); metacrawler.com;
msn.com; mus.com; nasa.gov; netscape.com; nfl.com; northernlight.com;
shop.com; winfiles.com; yellowpages.com

Every effort has been made to trace the copyright holders.
The publisher apologizes for any unintentional omissions and would be pleased,
in such cases, to place an acknowledgment in future editions of this book.